WISHING YOU THE VERY
BEST — NOW AND ALWAYS —

To Christy,

Wishing you the very
Best - Alex and Alwyn

The
Other Side
of Autumn

Selected Poems 1969 - 2022

DAVID PHIPPS

One Printers Way
Altona, MB R0G 0B0
Canada

www.friesenpress.com

Copyright © 2023 by David Phipps
First Edition — 2023

All rights reserved.

Scripture quotations taken from The Holy Bible, New International Version, NIV.

Copyright 1973, 1978, 1984, 2011 by Biblica, Inc.

Used by permission. All rights reserved worldwide.

No part of this publication may be reproduced in any form, or by any means, electronic or mechanical, including photocopying, recording, or any information browsing, storage, or retrieval system, without permission in writing from FriesenPress.

ISBN
978-1-03-916341-6 (Hardcover)
978-1-03-916340-9 (Paperback)
978-1-03-916342-3 (eBook)

1. POETRY, SUBJECTS & THEMES, INSPIRATIONAL & RELIGIOUS

Distributed to the trade by The Ingram Book Company

To my wife Jennifer, without whose help
and encouragement, these poems would
never have been published.

Autumn 5

The Struggle 7
Gethsemane 8
Sadness 9
Thanksgiving 10
A Tribute to Edwin Muir 11
Nothing Quite Equals 12
Roll That Stone 13
Life 14
Surrendering 16
Follow That Bright Star 17
Cold November Days 18
Epiphany 19
The Luncheon of the Boating Party
(My Dream) 21
Hope 22
November 23
Ritual 24
The Bench Engraving 25
The Simple Life 26

Winter ...27

Regret ... 29

Winter ... 30

Down ... 31

Let The Children Play ... 32

Child ... 33

Christmas ... 34

Safe ... 35

At The Beginning Of A New Year ... 36

A Thousand Miles ... 37

Unleashed ... 38

On Narcissism ... 39

If We Are So Advanced ... 40

Nightmare ... 41

Circle Of Love ... 42

Malice ... 44

Spring ...45

Good Friday ... 47

Easter ... 49

Risk ... 50

Surrounded ... 51

The Woman at the Well ... 52

Kichen ... 53

Today I Did Nothing ... 55

How Julie Nesrallah Saved My Bacon ... 56

The Goodness Of God ... 58

Step Backwards ... 59

Discovery By Anoesis ... 62

The Joys Of Growing Older ... 63

Only The Humble ... 64

Autumn

The Struggle

The pen is mightier than the knife.
That's what I've been told about life.
But let's examine it, you and me,
And see if we can solve it reasonably.
Both can wound and both can kill,
Just ask the hungry ones in the mill.
Tread slowly now, I'm down on one knee,
I'm entering waters of a different sea.
Both can raze the dusty ages,
It's just a history of warriors and sages.
I'm almost down for a count of three,
Can I conclude this successfully?
Yes; for only one can set you free.
Ask the children carving hearts on a tree.
Do you agree?
While I'm on this Earth,
This land,
These are the words by which I'll stand.

* This is the first poem I wrote while attending Queen's
University in 1969.

The Other Side of Autumn

Gethsemane

"They went to a place called Gethsemane."
—Mark 14:32

Have you been to the garden?
Have you wept the blood?
Have you suffered the anguish
Beyond and above?
Have you tasted the dust?
Have you felt the weight?
Have you seen the scars
And drunk the hate?

Finally you asked for the answer
And heard only reply,
Of silent stars in a still more silent sky.

David Phipps

Sadness

Never sadness stole like this
Into my wintered heart.
Never song signaled the end of bliss
As when the living part.

Never again can joy be so free
As in the youthful tide.
No! Now that I've tasted,
Have heard, do see,
Autumn's other side.

Thanksgiving

That utilitarian green.
(How very fatiguing by August!)
Has now become a cornucopia
Of crimson gold,
Gone wild in someone's creative imagination;
With breath so sharp, it shatters, like glass,
The unreality of summer slipped by.

I welcome you...
Despite your cool, standoffish manners,
You have a certain warmth about you.
So unlike the heat and haze
That sear the mind of man
And turn the truth into a lie.

Only Autumn is honest.
I embrace you...
Though your skin is cracked
And your branch is bare,
You have provided a rich harvest,
And for that,
I give thanks.

A Tribute to Edwin Muir

You didn't shy away from life
Under the year's assaults—
Through the battle, blood, and strife,
In the storm of good and bad,
You had the rare gift to express the sad
Exactly like Emily Brontë had.
Yes—the Scots know all about
The ills of body and soul.
A history steeped in courage and gall,
Of sinner, saint, and all.
"It's in the blood," I heard you say.
"To strive to make ourselves whole
Even when life is blow upon blow—
Smashed to bits by the Fall,
And each illusion of slippery peace
Is only chasing the wind."
Yet, "The world is a pleasant place,"
Softly you repeat…
On that day I'll never forget,
While the sun shone on your face,
Late summer in Princess Street.

The Other Side of Autumn

Nothing Quite Equals

Nothing quite equals a father's love;
Those who've had it know it's true;
Those denied, doubly so.
"But that's not true!" you say.

Then why the primal urge, the race,
The unquenchable drive,
The heartbreaking cry,
To finally rest in His embrace?

Roll That Stone

Roll that stone on up the hill,
Push it to the very top—
Then why in the name
Of all that's called sin,
Must I watch it roll down again?

If I had a nickel for all I've been told,
I'd be richer than Midas and Croesus combined;
And if I had a dime for every time
I've heard those lonely railcars clatter,
I'd buy that mansion bright.

So roll that stone on up the hill,
Push it to the very top-
Then why in the name
Of all that's called sin,
Must I watch it roll down again?

Life

Life's not just about doing well.
One grandfather worked in gold.
"Some things you must never sell,
But don't always do what you're told."

One grandfather worked in gold,
Another a man of the cloth.
"But don't always do what you're told,"
Where neither rust nor moth."

The other a man of the cloth,
Who rejoiced to study Greek,
Where neither rust nor moth,
"My child, what do you seek?"

Who rejoiced to study Greek;
The other made me a ring,
"My child, what do you seek?"
The other taught me to sing.

The other made me a ring,
Solid gold with the family crest.
The other taught me to sing,
"To give simple thanks is best."

David Phipps

Solid gold with the family crest.
"Some things you must never sell,
Sometimes more will lead to less."
Life's not just about doing well.

Surrendering

Surrendering to His love,
I fall into His arms
As warmth spreads through my body,
And calms my every fear.

Oh Father, why do I run away,
And push You from my life,
When all You're asking me to do,
Is let You draw me near?

David Phipps

Follow That Bright Star

Follow that bright star
Wherever it may lead,
But don't expect a palace—
Look instead for the straw-strewn barn.

Then allow your dreams to be crushed
And broken all apart—
"Abba, Father," then I prayed:
"I follow with all my heart."

Cold November Days

I like cold November days,
With just a tinge of regret;
Melancholy doesn't hurt either,
As I struggle to forget.

David Phipps

Epiphany

Every third Sunday we go
And volunteer for a small service.
Honestly, I don't want to go,
And flip through my excuses Rolodex -
But then end up going anyway.

Our first job is to collect the residents
And quickly wheel them down to the chapel.
"Would you like to come to church today?"
"Sure, why not." Or, "Not today."
Or cold blank stare.

The smell is the first thing that engulfs you,
Slapping and smacking you around
With your own personal wake up call,
Mixed with burnt cheese sandwiches
And assorted bodily fluids.

Each room, about the size of a janitorial cubicle,
Has a mini glass box outside the door.
It's filled with pictures of happier times,
Youth and sun, beaches and family,
Love and desire.
I stare through the reflection, always struck
By the way time and life
Has sifted and scythed them down

The Other Side of Autumn

Like a plastic surgeon's skillful scalpel,
Until they're finally
completely unrecognizable—
Cleverly disguised with a slice, a wound,
a heartache.

Always glad to leave, I rush home through
the storm
And luxuriate in the comforting warmth
and peace.
But that night, peering into my own glass box,
I'm suddenly startled and shocked to discover,
I'm also being swiftly cut down to size.

The Luncheon of
the Boating Party
(My Dream)

The art expert droned on and on
As a fat fly buzzed
In ever diminishing circles.
"Note the spatial telescoping—Pere Fournaise
Is much larger than his daughter,
Who in turn is much larger than his son.
Diversity of hue is richly saturated
While adjacent complimentaries
Flicker in solidarity of form..."

"No!" I shouted.
"The four yellow hats with the white linen cloth
Are the key to unlock the mystery...
How Renoir conjured up that perfect climax
To a perfect day—
Those last few happy minutes
Before it's time to go,
And thoughts must drift (they have no choice),
To accounts payable,
Impossible relationships,
And sad responsibilities."

The Other Side of Autumn

Hope

I am a creature of hope.
I am like you—
One who needs to see that glimmer of light
At the window of my cell.
When I'm crawling like a lizard
Through the repetition of empty days,
Groping from place to place
Only to find each one drier than the last—
Friend, that's when I need to hear
A word of hope.
Even if spoken by halting, clay lips
Like my own.

And when my God seems as far away
As that star that's only blinking,
And my faith has ceased to beat—
When thoughts that once inspired dreams
Now only return to mock—
Friend, that's when I need to feel
A hand reach out,
And with one gentle touch
Vault my spirit over these walls
That are closing in around me.

I am a creature of hope—
I am like you.

November

Now darker days and nights invade
To cast their long, more sinister shades
That warn of things already past,
And things to come—
While swiftly changing clouds
Form cryptic Delphic omens.
What prophetic word then!? What insight!?

Come then, and tramp with me
Through the sullen, greying woods.
October, her sister, has fled,
And no golden strands remain.

Ask November any question you want.
Just don't expect a reply.

The Other Side of Autumn

Ritual

Put one foot in front of the other.
Yes, I know it sounds trite,
But it's often the way to survive
In life's continual fight.

David Phipps

The Bench Engraving

Come rest a while with me.
Life's fleeting hour is passing.
Yes, it's certainly a lonely spot,
But please, sit down anyway.

I also chased that golden ring
Of slippery success,
Conquering every mountain
As I strove to be the best;

No—let the world steamroller on
With all its vain pursuits,
But you—
You rest a while with me.

The Other Side of Autumn

The Simple Life

The simple life is not the easy life,
Despite what people say.
Yes, many a ship has run aground,
Seeking that golden day.

Multitudes hear that Siren call,
And drift away off course,
Only to finally discover that,
To live the simple life…
Is really the hardest life of all.

David Phipps

Winter

Regret

It stood by the edge of the woods.
Shadowy figure, or shadow itself,
I could not tell.
All I know is that it was strange,
And we prefer the familiar,
The ordinary, the dull.
I quickly drew my knife, and
Ran.
But that was long ago.
Now, white with age,
I often wonder with regret—
Did it also run?

Winter

Foolish Winter!
To think that you could stay forever.
Your iron grip has been broken
By the gentle Spring.

Proud and boastful at year's beginning,
You're drunk with power and show no mercy,
As you pierce all your enemies with icy spears.
Yet no sign of you now remains.

How stupid of you to brag in December,
When April shows so clearly
What a liar you are!

David Phipps

Down

Down, down, down
Falls the heavy heart,
Crushed from cradle's cries
And screaming nightmare eyes.
Lost in darkness, each step leads
To know how pain in silence breeds.
And then the heart becomes a stone,
Tied round the neck
To swing alone.

Let The Children Play

Let the children play!
Their sunshine laughter twirling
round and round and round—
Taking them to joyful places
Only they will ever know.
Let the children play!
Soon enough will come the day
Of grey concern—
Banging on the door
To leave a bag of burdens,
To toss and turn with,
On creaking springs.

David Phipps

Child

Beautiful Child,
Thou most Holy!
Have you come, then,
To wrestle back a kingdom
From a crib!?

Oh Child,
Surely you know not the forces you fight,
Or you would have come with strength
And stealth. Yes,
Wise in the things of this world—
Not as a nursing babe!

Your eyes, so soft,
What can they know of deceit?
And will a smile
Defeat a fortressed foe?

How can you then look at me
With such calm, assuring peace?
When just one heavy blow of a fist
Would cause your breath to cease?

Beautiful Child,
Thou most Holy!
This mystery I cannot grasp,
As I worship in the straw and dung.

The Other Side of Autumn

Christmas

Lord, this year I pray,
Don't let the tinsel get in the way.
Those twinkling lights so clear and bright
Can easily hide the Child's sight.
Gift upon gift, packages piled high,
And lofty thoughts about the meaning of it all.
Lord, don't let these things distract me
From my desperate need of Thee!
And Lamb of God, you friend of the
broken hearted,
Amidst all this laughter, mirth and song,
May I taste (but a little)
The ache you wrestled with
From before the world's foundation,
As Time held its breath, and all became still,
Your Father asked you that agonizing question -
And you quietly replied,
"I will."

David Phipps

Safe

Safe in His arms,
Here I'll stay,
Loved by Him today.

At The Beginning
Of A New Year

Why do we love to sit
And watch the snowflakes fall?
Perhaps because it reminds us
We're not really in control at all.
We secretly delight in drift and moan
So we can pretend we're all alone
And all safe paths are gone.

That night our dreams are deep and long,
And all we're really praying for
Is a clean white sheet -
To write something on.

David Phipps

A Thousand Miles

A thousand miles an hour
Our jeweled planet flies,
Yet we never ask
How or why.
Shouldn't we at least stop and think
Why our brains have this missing link?

Unleashed

> In Chaos Theory, "the Butterfly Effect"
> is the
> sensitive dependence on initial conditions
> in which a small change in one state can
> result in large differences in a later state.

I awoke; and was, quite frankly,
Surprised to find the world still here!
So sure that my blistering rage last night
Had suddenly morphed into a conflagration,
That had finally engulfed the whole wide world.
That my tongue—freely flapping up and down
Like mutating butterfly wings—
Had somehow pressed someone's hot buttons
At a subterranean silo somewhere
in Nebraska...
I luxuriated in the relief
That only nightmare wakers know—
And then, rolling over, I fell back asleep,
To slumber on again.

On Narcissism

Mirror, Mirror, on the wall,
Who's the fairest of them all?
I only see one image there...
And so it must be me.

Cruel it surely must be
When we come to believe it's true!
But ingrained from birth it is,
And so we have no problem
Succumbing to this.

But if we think the world
Is revolving just for us,
We never learn the secrets
Of sacrificial love.

We mightily toil in the strong delusion
That all must eventually come to see
Just how wonderful and special
Is little old me.

The Other Side of Autumn

If We Are So Advanced

If we are so advanced,
As everyone gloats,
Then why are we still
At each other's throats?

Surely billions of brain leaps
Should have eliminated by now,
Our bloody desire
To slaughter each other,
Brother.

Nightmare

I dreamt the world had ended,
And all lay hushed and still;
But a bitter rain kept falling
Upon the final two.

The Other Side of Autumn

Circle Of Love

"If I had but one regret
T'would be that I could not love
Only you as the cherished one;
But If I had to make it two
T'would be that unforgiveness bitter;
But then, why not make it three?"

"Some say the charm is lucky three,
But having never tasted of regret,
You know so little of real bitter,
The suffering required of stilted love,
The circled chain that's only two,
But breakable by the careless one.
How could you spurn me for another
Now that we are a union of three
And it's no longer just us two?"

"Life is too short to be ruled by regret;
Come, let's drink our fill of love—
Your sorry state is making me bitter."

"Don't talk to me of sour and bitter,
By this our hearts will never be one;
Swear to me now your sacred love,
And acknowledge this circle of three.
Life should not be one long regret
Think more of me now, one become two."

David Phipps

"I can't stand this jail of two;
Each day becomes more dour and bitter;
And my heart is filled with cold regret…
But I forbid you to have more than me,
Though it will please me to have three.
Come on, let's drink our fill of love."

"Then I too will play this game of love;
I'll also shatter this chain of two.
I'll outdo you by six to three
Until your bones will leak the bitter;
And soon I won't be the only one
Living in this drear regret."

"So we both regret our withered love.
Was it one thing or was it two?
No—it was the bitter that consumed all three."

The Other Side of Autumn

Malice

O you black Snake!
Who with your brother Tongue
Can wreck such havoc!
And meanwhile, your sister Gossip
Just loves to see
The complete and total ruin
One single word can do!

David Phipps

Spring

Good Friday

> "When the soldiers had crucified Jesus,
> they divided his clothes." — John 19:23

We were careful to guard our shares that day—
Four neat little piles.
It seemed important at the time.
This was our bonus, and why not?
A soldier's life is hard at the best of times.

Another day, another dollar—
That's the way I looked at it.
Then I suggested the dice, because, you know,
A seamless garment is worth a lot,
And God knows, things weren't getting any
less expensive.
We had to get through that bloody awful
day somehow,
And cheap wine and risky living
Had always worked before.
But this day was different.

Looking back now, it all seems so pointless,
Like climbing the rungs of a ladder—
Going nowhere,
Scratching and clawing our way to the very
Bottom.

The Other Side of Autumn

What could we have possibly done with our
little treasures?
Sewn them into robes of righteousness?
Woven them into a crown of glory?
How could we have been that close
To touching the hem of His garment,
And then frittered it all away?
It seemed important at the time.

David Phipps

Easter

> "And I will put enmity between you
> and the woman, and between your
> seed and her seed; he will crush your
> head, and you will strike his heel." —
> Genesis 3:15

The devil is afraid of seeds.
Yes, those little things so small
You can hardly see
What earthly good a seed could be.
For he knows that one kept to itself
Will never cause him any harm,
But if it finds some soil to grow,
Like something buried in a grave below,
All hell will shriek out its alarm!
For he can't forget, try as he will,
The Seed he thought for sure was dead
That suddenly germinated and crushed his head.
So never despise the tiny things that you plant;
God realizes their potential, even if you can't.

The Other Side of Autumn

Risk

Race against time.
Is the gamble worth the gain?
Was peace ever made without struggle,
Or substance without pain?

The farmer falters,
And strains to hear reply
As thunder crashes
And warnings light the sky.

Surrounded

> "Do this in remembrance of me."
> —Luke 22:19

Surrounded by all I've achieved,
Surely nothing can touch me now.
Until the bread and wine are served.
Yes, they cut me,
And how strange my dream last night!
Stairways, and stones, and striving,
The always wrestling
For that elusive blessing.
How black that night was!

But then I awoke to a burst of light—
And a delicious sea breeze rolling in,
That slowly blew those shabby curtains
Farther and farther apart.

The Woman at the Well

> When a Samaritan women came to draw
> water, Jesus said to her, "Will you give me
> a drink?" —John 4:7

She went slowly down to Jacob's well
To quench her thirst at scorching noon,
But in her sadness she did dwell.

A man was resting—something to sell?
The sun beat down on perpetual ruin.
She went slowly down to Jacob's well.

"Where should we worship? Who can tell?"
Only a prophet…or a crazy loon!
But in her sadness she did dwell.

"Living waters—"that rings a bell.
Maybe I could sing a different tune."
She went slowly down to Jacob's well.

"Come see a man who seemed to be able
To read my heart like an ancient rune."
And her sadness he did quell.

The whole village then sent up a yell.
"What a strange gift! We're over the moon!"
She went slowly down to Jacob's well,
And her sadness he did quell.

David Phipps

Kichen

> A pidgin language used by servants
> and employers to communicate
> more easily.

Do family members and many guests
Tend to congregate
In your kitchen?

Then make it large
Enough to accommodate
Plenty of seating space.

Do you approve of or insist
On having meals other than breakfast
In your kitchen?

Then you had better plan
An efficient layout,
With space for a table.

What are your shopping habits?
If you prefer extended periods of time
between shopping,
You will need ample storage space.

Remember to provide
Adequate working space
For the many guests,

The Other Side of Autumn

And sufficient counter space,
With a large island
For those who congregate.

All kitchens must contain cabinets
Beneath the sink
For canned or packaged goods.

Analyze your shopping habits again
If you prefer an efficient layout
For long periods.

Today I Did Nothing

Don't just do something,
Stand there.

Today I did nothing,
It was really quite grand;
No texting, no email, no Facebook for sure—
Oh that darn social media vice!

No, I sat on my deck
With a coffee in hand,
And thought of this strange mysterious life,
So often filled with bitter strife.

Oh if we could only slow down,
And get off that bullet train somehow…
Then perhaps we could occasionally smile,
Or heaven forbid,
Actually laugh once in a while.

The Other Side of Autumn

How Julie Nesrallah
Saved My Bacon

It all started with a renovation…
(It always does.)
Why, why do I take these jobs with
perfectionist women?
It must be my fear of not having enough.
You know—of running out of greenbacks,
Lettuce, rhinos, frog skins, rivets.
I just can't afford to turn a job down.
Then throw in two hyperactive Cocker Spaniels,
And again, the howling
existential question… why?

I recently read an article in National Geographic
That said that risk takers have more dopamine
Attached to their auto receptors.
The payoff is that your system is
Flooded with the stuff
When you reach your goal.
Looking back, now, this must be another reason
Why I take these jobs.

David Phipps

One hour into my Arctic exploration,
She said,
"Would you like a radio to listen to?"
I almost refused, but there must have been
An angel watching over me.
From the very first notes, I knew I had found
My survival rations.
"Bring it on," I almost shouted one day
In the middle of Ludwig's Walstein,
With its lovely 'catch me if you can' notes.
"Be as fussy britches as you want,
Nobody's knocking me off my tightrope today!"

So thank you, Julie Nesrallah.
And thank you, dopamine.

The Goodness Of God

The goodness of God still cascades down
Like flashes from the sun—
It plunges, it oozes, it fills
Every crevice, every nook.
Oh traveler, won't you look?

It slowly drips from the old winepress
On hot and languid days.
It waterfalls and does cartwheels
Down every lonely street.
It cries out at the crossroads
And sings by the babbling brook.
Oh traveler, won't you look?

David Phipps

Step Backwards

One day I received an old black and white
From sixty long years ago.
And suddenly, nostalgia floods my soul.
Grade one 1955...
With prim and proper Miss Beck,
Carefully shepherding her flock.

Now I imagine that all of us
Have some primitive connection to our
first teacher;
Not that we understood all the implications,
of course,
But somehow we knew we'd begun
To slowly orbit another star, and to
Fall beneath its gravitational pull.
Yes, we were glad to get away
From our mother's iron grip for a while,
But equally happy to run home again.

I remember that sunny winter's day
When Bill Skinner (God bless him)
Stuck his hot 98.6 degree tongue
Against the -10 steel swing frame.
He bawled like a baby calf, until Miss Beck
Brought a cup of warm water to procure
his release,

The Other Side of Autumn

Scolding him terribly.
"Something there is that doesn't like us"
Someone once wrote,
And I believe it!

Immediately behind the swings were the woods,
With their mysterious unchartered paths.
Did I say woods? 100 sq. yards, tops.
Paths? 3 at the most.
But to a young boy, they were
adventure's promise,
The faint hope, that one way or the other,
Life's rigid structure could be counterbalanced—
If we could just solve the equation.
My friend Peter said there were
Wolves that roamed there at night,
But we never dared to find out.

The young faces stare back at me.
The girls already light-years ahead socially,
Bonding and connecting
On some unfathomable level.
The boys unsure, hesitant, awkward.
Me? I'm stuck in the back row
Beside the tallest girl in the class.

David Phipps

My only consolation that day
(as far as I can see),
Is that I'm just one backwards step away
From those lovely, shaded paths.

Discovery By Anoesis

Anoesis: Consciousness that is
pure passive receptiveness without
understanding or intellectual organization
of the material presented.

"For anyone who speaks in a tongue does
not speak to people but to God. Indeed,
no one understands them; they express
mysteries by the Spirit."
I Corinthians 14:2

I seek, I chase, I knock,
My mind cascading in tongues
Like crazy subatomic lottery balls
That dart and dance encased.

Then, suddenly, one drops,
And I hear that beautiful click
That tells me I've hit the jackpot.
My ship has finally come in!

Oh, that sweet windfall, aha!
Somehow made my day,
That soon I felt so rich
I gave it all away.

David Phipps

The Joys Of Growing Older

I don't have to check my phone
I don't have to be on time
I can spend my whole day
Composing rhyme.

I don't have to check emails
I don't have to diet
I can finally rest all day
And find some peace and quiet.

I don't have to answer texts
Or jump when the boss says jump
OAS tops up my account
Now that's a real fist-pump!

Yes, it's true, my dentures hurt
And what the heck's that pain?
But all things considered, add it up
The loss can't compare to the gain.

Only The Humble

Only the humble survive
To fight another day.
The proud get so brittle,
To dust they decay.

Only the proud will never see,
The reason for their sighs;
But the humble perceive it,
And fall, to fail, to rise.

David Phipps

Printed in Canada